The 90s, The Last Offline Generation

A nostalgic ride through the digital transformation

Soumya Viswanathan

The 90s, The Last Offline Generation
A nostalgic ride through the digital transformation

First Edition, Version 1.0
17 Dec, 2025

Published by Soumya Viswanathan

Dedicated to-
all those who grew up in the '90s.

Contents

Chapter 1: Introduction 1
Chapter 2: From Doordarshan to OTTs..........................3
Chapter 3: From Cassettes to Streaming Playlists 9
Chapter 4: From Akashavani to News Feeds 15
Chapter 5: From Brick Games to Play-station 23
Chapter 6: From Photo Albums to Cloud storage 29
Chapter 7: From Booth calls to Video Calls.................35
Chapter 8: From Human Guides to Digital Maps 45
Chapter 9: From Browsing Centres to Wi-fi 51
Chapter 10: From Local Offices to Online Portals 59
Chapter 11: From Shops to Online Shopping..............67
Chapter 12: From Ticket Counters to Online Booking 73
Chapter 13: From Auto Stands to Algorithmic Rides ..81
Chapter 14: From Floor trading to Online trading 87
Chapter 15: From Encyclopaedias to AI Prompts 95
Chapter 16: From Casual Lessons to Coaching class.105
Chapter 17: From Textbooks to Visual Learning 113
Chapter 18: Conclusion...119

FOREWARD

by Sweta Samota

Some generations are shaped by disruption.
Others are shaped by transition.

The 90s generation belongs to the rare few who lived fully in both worlds—the slow, tangible, offline world and the fast, invisible, digital one. We remember a time before notifications demanded our attention, before memories were stored in clouds instead of cupboards, and before conversations were interrupted by screens.

The 90s: The Last Offline Generation is a gentle return to that world.

As someone who has spent years working with stories—my own and those of thousands of authors—I believe that the most powerful stories are not always dramatic or extraordinary. Often, they are found in the ordinary moments we once lived without realising their value. Soumya Viswanathan understands this deeply.

This book does not romanticise the past or resist the present. Instead, it does something far more meaningful—it helps us **pause at the bridge between two eras**. The handwritten notes, STD booths, Doordarshan evenings, Akashavani voices, Kodak cameras, and unhurried conversations are not just memories; they are markers of a way of being that shaped our patience, attention, relationships, and inner lives.

What makes this book special is its emotional honesty. It recognises that while technology has brought speed and convenience, something quieter was lost along the way—presence. And the 90s generation carries that memory in its bones.

This book will resonate with those who grew up in the 90s, help parents reflect on the world they came from, and offer younger readers a glimpse into a life lived with fewer distractions and deeper connections.

As you turn these pages, I invite you not just to read—but to remember. To smile at moments, you thought you had forgotten. And to recognise how that offline world still quietly lives within you.

— Sweta Samota
Author • TEDx Speaker • Book Coach
Founder, India Authors Academy

PREFACE

Growing up in the '90s meant belonging to a world that no longer exists, a world that moved slower, breathed softer, and held warmth in ways today's world often forgets. We were the last ones to experience childhood without screens, without notifications buzzing beside us, without the invisible pressure of being available all the time.

My childhood, and perhaps yours too was built around waiting.
Waiting for Sundays to watch a movie.
Waiting for cassettes to rewind.
Waiting for film rolls to develop.
Waiting in queues to make a phone call.
Waiting for handwritten letters that travelled slowly but carried emotions more honestly than any emoji ever could.

Somewhere in that waiting, life felt fuller — richer — more meaningful.

This book is not about technology or its evolution. It is about us, **the last offline generation** and **the first online generation**.

We were the teenagers who navigated life without Google, the families who gathered around a single TV, the friends whose secrets that lived only in conversations and disappeared into the air, not into screenshots.

We were the bridge generation.

One foot in the slow, analogue world and the other

stepping into the fast, digital one. We grew up with landlines and lived long enough to watch mobile phones become extensions of ourselves. We used floppy disks and then adapted to pen drives. We saw the internet arrive like a distant miracle and then take over every corner of life.

The nostalgia we carry is not just for the objects but for the emotions attached to them.
A cassette wasn't merely music, it was effort, patience, and joy.
A photo wasn't just an image; it was a moment captured after careful thought.
A video game wasn't a distraction; it was a shared memory with siblings and cousins.

Through this book, I want to take you back gently, not to glorify the past but to remember how it shaped us. To revisit the simplicity we lived in, the patience we built without knowing, the togetherness we didn't even realize we were blessed with. As you turn each chapter, I hope it awakens memories resting quietly somewhere within you.

This is not a history of the '90s.

It is a feeling.
A feeling of who we were before the world sped up.
A feeling of what we carry even today in our habits, in our nostalgia, in the small ways we still crave simplicity.

This book is for everyone who lived through the transition who remembers life before the scroll.
It is a tribute to the shift we witnessed, the changes we adapted to, and the quiet strength of being shaped by two worlds.

We gained a lot.
We lost a lot.
And somewhere in between, we became who we are today.

Let's step back in time slowly, one chapter at a time.

Acknowledgement

Writing this book has been a journey back through time, and I could not have walked through those memories alone.

Special thanks to Sweta Samota, my mentor, whose guidance, encouragement, and insightful advice shaped this book at every step. Her support helped me navigate my thoughts, refine my ideas, and turn memories into words. I am also grateful to the Likhega India Mission 2025 for inspiring this work.

I am grateful to everyone who shaped the world. I grew up in a world of slowness, simplicity, and shared moments that became the foundation of this work.

To my family and friends, who shaped my life for who I am today. The stories, the warmth, and the way of living taught me the value of connection long before technology changed our lives.

To my husband, who shares his part of this journey too, thank you for the memories we continue to create, the perspectives you bring, and the quiet support that stays steady in the background of everything I write.

A Special mention to my sister, who stepped into the pages for my sake, even though books aren't her world, and still offered her thoughtful feedback.

I also want to thank the readers who carry the same nostalgia, and the same quiet longing for the life we once knew.

And finally, thank you to the digital world itself for showing me the contrast, the transition, and the story hidden between two eras. Without that shift, this book would have had no meaning.

This book is a tribute to all of us who lived through the change. There may be many moments from your own life that are not written here, but I hope these pages awaken those unwritten memories resting quietly within you.

Thank you for being part of this journey.

Chapter 1: Introduction

If you grew up in the '90s, then you, like me, have lived two lives in one lifetime.

We grew up in a world where Sundays meant waiting for a movie on Doordarshan, where cameras had limited film and every photograph mattered, where letters took days or weeks to reach, and where one landline connected an entire household and sometimes the neighbourhood.

And then, almost without warning, we watched the world switch on.

Suddenly, everything we needed, music, maps, money, messages, memories fit inside a screen small enough to hold in our palms.

We didn't just watch the world change.
We adapted to it.
We learned it.
We stumbled, resisted, embraced, and evolved with it.

From rotary phones to ringtones, from letters to OTPs, from diaries to passwords, our lifetime witnessed one of the greatest transitions in history.

We learned the internet the same way we learned life. Slowly, curiously, and sometimes clumsily.

We watched search bars replace elders' wisdom, playlists replace mixtapes, and Wi-Fi quietly replace everything.

This book is a nostalgic ride through that transformation.

A reminder of the days when boredom wasn't a problem, it was normal. When childhood wasn't online, it was lived outside. When every digital "first" felt magical- the first email, the first ringtone, the first online payment.

We are the last offline generation.

And this is our story of innocence, transition, confusion, excitement, and everything in between.

For younger readers, this book is a window, a glimpse into a world before notifications dictated our day.
Each chapter is a standalone memory. Together, they trace the timeline of a generation that grew up before the scroll, and now lives inside it.

Welcome to this journey.
Welcome back to that world.
Welcome to our story, from offline to online.

Chapter 2: From Doordarshan to OTTs

There was a time when a single television in one house could unite an entire neighbourhood. One home, usually the wealthier one became the unofficial cinema hall. Cricket matches, Sunday movies, news bulletins, and mythological serials were not just entertainment; they were events.

People walked in unannounced, children squeezed into floor corners, aunties exchanged gossips, and uncles argued over commentary as if the cricketers could hear them. Some days we were welcomed warmly, other days we felt like we had entered without permission, but we still stayed, because missing the match wasn't an option.

Slowly, televisions multiplied. Every home had one. But even then, it was "the television", not "your television". One screen, one timetable that everyone obeyed. There was no debate like today's "What should we watch?" The only question was, "What is coming now?"

And somehow, that simplicity worked.

Doordarshan had its own rhythm. Programmes weren't just shows, they became timekeepers. The Doordarshan signature tune was the official start of the evening. News hour meant silence, whether we liked it or not. Weekly serials were eagerly anticipated, and Sunday movies could stop an entire town. If our family had guests visiting during the Sunday movie slot, we secretly hoped they would leave early, not because we disliked them, but because priorities were priorities.

The antenna on the terrace deserves an honourable mention. One person stood on the roof turning it inch by inch, while another shouted instruction from the balcony "Left… right… no no—go back! Yes! Stop!" That was our version of Wi-Fi troubleshooting.

In those days, entertainment was a shared emotion. If someone missed an episode due to a wedding, a journey, or worst of all, a power cut, they relied on neighbours for a full recap. Spoilers weren't considered rude; they were community service.

Life was slow. Entertainment was limited. But perhaps that limitation made everything feel precious.

Then change arrived, not suddenly, but quietly at first.

Cable TV entered our living rooms, bringing a flood of channels. Sun Network, Gemini, Udaya, Surya, Asianet for the South, Cartoon Network for the kids, MTV and Sony TV for teenagers, Star Sports for sports lovers. The menu of entertainment expanded overnight. But the battle shifted from "What is coming?" to "Who has the remote?"

Remote-control fights became legendary. If someone changed the channel without warning, the entire family reacted instantly. Advertisements became scheduled bathroom breaks. The living room transformed into a shared battlefield of preferences.

Soon came VCRs, CDs, and DVDs. Renting a movie or cassette was an event, complete with reviews from the shop owner, who behaved like a film critic. Watching a rented movie felt earned, because there were a return deadline and late fees. We ensured we watched it before the deadline.

But change didn't stop there.

A computer entered the home, usually kept in a corner, treated like a delicate museum piece. The dial-up internet screeching tone became the background music of curiosity. Then, one day, YouTube arrived.

Entertainment was shifting from collective to individual.

Then arrived the three-letter revolution: **OTT**. (Over the top)

When we first heard the term, most of us didn't know what it meant. Netflix felt foreign. Hotstar was just for cricket. Amazon Prime was something that came free with delivery benefits. We didn't subscribe because we wanted OTT, we subscribed because someone said, "There's a free trial."

But slowly, quietly, it became a habit.

Suddenly, we could pause. Rewind. Skip ads. Watch an entire season in a night. Watch in the car, on the bed, on the balcony, during lunch, during travel and everywhere. Entertainment was no longer tied to a room or schedule.

And that changed everything.

Password sharing became the modern equivalent of lending DVDs. Typing movie names into search bars felt serious like filling an exam form. Algorithms started predicting what we might like better than our own family. The remote control lost its throne and touchscreens took over.

One day, without even noticing, the shift completed.

Television became the background noise. OTT became the default.

Today, every person has their own screen, their own preference, their own playlist of dramas, documentaries, stand-up shows, reality TV, and films. The same roof now shelters separate viewing worlds. Parents watch spiritual programmes, serials, reality shows or news debates. Teenagers binge Korean dramas or thrillers. Children live inside YouTube and cartoons. The question is no longer, "What are we watching?" but "What are you watching?"

Homes became quieter. Screens became louder.

And somewhere along the way, we lost small things like collective laughter, the thrill of waiting for Sunday premieres, the shared shock when a plot twist unfolded, the ritual of everyone sitting together at the exact same time.

Yet, in a strange way, we carry both eras inside us.

We remember the slow charm of the static screen, the antenna struggles, the shared curiosity of watching something for the first time in unison. We also live in the fast convenience of the autoplay, the skip intro, the binge-watch marathon.

Perhaps that is what makes our generation unique. We didn't just witness the change. We lived it.

We transitioned from national routines to personal choices.
From collective consumption to curated algorithms.
From one scheduled programme to unlimited content.

And somewhere deep inside, despite the luxury of having endless entertainment in our pockets, we still smile when we hear the old Doordarshan tune or when we see a vintage TV with a curved screen and antenna.

Not because we miss the shows.
But because we miss the innocence.

A time when entertainment required waiting. When watching meant sharing space. When stories weren't consumed and they were experienced together.

And now, as we scroll through endless options at midnight, unable to choose what to watch, a small part of us longs for the simplicity of turning on the TV and accepting whatever appeared.

No skip intro.
No suggestions.
No algorithm.

Just us.
Just the moment.
Just enough.

We grew through both worlds, and maybe that balance is our quiet superpower.

Growing up in both worlds made us realize how much has changed not just in technology, but in the way we connect, navigate, and explore.

We remember waiting, not just for pages to load, but for our turn, for a chair, for time.
Asking strangers, "Excuse me, is your system done?"

We remember a world without passwords.
We remember a world where internet meant planning.
We have walked to browsing centres, and now scroll from bed.
We remember a time when screens were scarce and conversations were abundant.
We remember a time before Wi-Fi, before "Airplane Mode," before "Connect Automatically."
We remember a time before "Wi-fi password please.."

As we grew up across two technological timelines, they gave us a rare gift: perspective.

We know real maps and Google Maps.
We know floppy disks and cloud drives.
We know Orkut testimonials and Instagram stories.

We learned life through trial, error, clicking, waiting, and adapting.

Maybe that is what makes our generation interesting, not just what we experienced, but everything we transitioned through.

So even as we enjoy the ease of today's world, a small part of us still smiles thinking of the past.

Yet we thrive in a world where everything is one tap away.

We didn't just learn technology, we grew alongside it, stumbled with it, and shaped it while it shaped us.

Maybe that journey itself is our generation's real password.

A secret, only we remember.

Chapter 10: From Local Offices to Online Portals

There was a time when getting any government work done meant stepping out with a folder of documents, a pen, and a deep breath.

Local Government offices and banks were once physical destinations we mentally prepared for. People woke up early, packed water bottles and snacks, gathered photocopies, and carried passport-size photos like currency. Some carried extra glue, some carried staplers, and some carried the confidence of having faced that office before. Everyone travelled with the same hopeful thought running through their minds: "Maybe the work gets done today".

Before technology simplified everything, life had its own rhythm. Electricity bills and water bills were stacked neatly. Property tax receipts, PAN acknowledgments, land documents, LIC premium cards, everything belonged to a physical drawer or a metal file that snapped shut with a stubborn clip. Every family had a labelled folder with documents arranged chronologically, protected like treasure.

These documents weren't just paperwork. They marked milestones. A ration card meant inclusion. A voter ID meant identity. A bank passbook filled with blue-ink entries felt worthy of celebration. The small stamps, the scribbled dates, the stapled corners everything had a strangely emotional weight. They weren't just records; they were proof of progress.

And then, there were **money orders**, a chapter many still smile remembering.

Sending money was not a quick transaction on a screen. It was a process, we filled out a money order form, carefully wrote the receiver's name and address, counted cash twice, and handed it to a postal clerk who stamped it with authority. Days later, the postman arrived, often greeted like a messenger of joy.

Sometimes, he delivered money.
Sometimes, he delivered handwritten notes attached, birthday wishes, festival blessings, congratulations, or just a simple: **"Take care."**

Receiving a money order meant something more than funds. It meant someone remembered us. It was emotional currency wrapped in bureaucracy. People would sign the receipt with gratitude and sometimes even give the postman a small tip, a tradition that briefly turned banking into a human celebration.

Back then, even withdrawing money meant visiting the bank, signing withdrawal slips, updating passbooks, waiting in queues, and listening to soft conversations mixed with the rhythmic stamping of documents. Patience was part of the transaction.

Standing in queues wasn't just waiting, it was participation in a very human system. Strangers became advisors. Elderly people shared wisdom about which counter worked faster. Some explained rules, some shared stories, and some just complained about how things were better or worse before. Everyone exchanged the same expression repeatedly, a half-tired, half-hopeful smile.

And when our turn finally arrived, there was a ceremony to it. We placed our documents on the table with cautious optimism. If the officer stamped and signed without questions, it felt like a victory. If they sent us back for one missing photocopy or photograph, the day turned into a new adventure with another queue, another photocopier, another chance.

Filling out forms, paying dues, submitting documents these mundane acts, often overlooked, carry their own subtle weight. The process of visiting offices, facing challenges along the way, taking leaves and permissions from work, and navigating the small hurdles of daily life, all of it leaves its mark. Each document holds a story worth telling.

Walking out of the office with a stamped, signed document or the work done felt like the system had acknowledged our existence. It wasn't just a task completed; it was an achievement.

And then came the **Aadhaar** — a turning point disguised as an ID.

Suddenly entire cities saw queues again, but this time not to submit forms rather, to give fingerprints, iris scans, and personal details to a new identity system. People stood outside schools, banks, temples, community halls anywhere Aadhaar enrolment teams set up computers. The process felt futuristic and unfamiliar.

For the first time, identity wasn't just a document, it was biometric.

No more carrying multiple proofs. No more confusion about which ID counted. Aadhaar promised one number that could hold it all, identity, address, proof, authentication and all stored quietly inside a database instead of a file folder.

Once Aadhaar integrated itself into daily life, everything else accelerated. Passbooks went digital. Authentication became instant. OTPs replaced physical signatures. The long walk from counter to counter turned into scrolling, selecting and uploading.

At First, offices introduced computers. Then, websites. Then, portals. It all seemed optional just another way to "avoid crowds."

But slowly, forms disappeared from counters. Token systems replaced queues. Online appointments replaced early-morning lineups.

People started downloading forms instead of collecting them. Help desks slowly replaced long corridors. The officer's signature turned into digital verification. The stamp turned into a QR code. It was not a sudden change. It was a series of small changes, so steady that one day we looked back and realized the office we knew had become a place we barely visited anymore.

Nobody expected this shift to be so permanent.

And soon, the familiar journey to the local office became unnecessary.

The tax filings, electricity bills, PAN-Aadhaar linking, certificates, passport updates, health insurance, life insurance, school admissions, pension verification, banking all living inside screens, apps, logins, passwords, biometric authentication, and confirmation emails.

Earlier we asked, "Which counter?"
Now we ask, "Which portal?" or "Which app?"

Earlier we took token numbers.
Now we wait for OTPs.

Earlier we checked forms twice.
Now we check if the PDF is under 2 MB.

Everything works faster almost too fast. Tasks that once carried emotional weight now vanish into silent digital completion. The struggle that once taught patience has now turned into expectation.

Today, almost everything happens online. The Complaints, applications, renewals, and what not.

Somewhere between those long queues and instant OTPs, an entire lifestyle changed quietly, but completely.

The system is cleaner.
Faster.
More predictable.
No need to apply leave from work, no need to

travel, no need to stand in queues that move like glaciers.

But it is also quieter.
Queues have mostly disappeared, replaced by apps and notifications. All the bills and taxes can now be paid under UPI, just a few taps away.

The rhythm of waiting in crowded offices has shifted to the quiet hum of phones, yet the small victories remain: a payment confirmed, a receipt downloaded, a task completed.

Even in this digital ease, there is a subtle satisfaction in knowing the mundane has been managed, and life continues its steady pulse.

Everything is efficient, almost too efficient.
The emotional weight of "getting something done" has dissolved into a soft click on a screen.

Convenience won again.

This shift reflects something bigger than paperwork. It shows how our generation lived between two worlds:

One world where work meant showing up.
Another where work means logging in.

One world filled with humans, noise, confusion, and shared experiences.
Another, clicking "Submit" while sipping tea.

Online portals are becoming more smooth, fast, and reliable.

Still, there is something beautiful about having lived between these two eras.
We remember government seals and QR codes. We remember signatures and biometric authentication.

We are the generation that stood in queues and later learned to refresh browsers.

Because convenience can change our routine, but memory keeps reminding us of the world, where getting one signature or paying a bill felt like a story worth telling.

Yet, even today, the old world hasn't vanished completely. There are still places where forms are printed, queues wind slowly, and people wait with uncertainty.

Some portals freeze in between, some apps crash, some passwords never work when we need them most. And, we have to redo the entire process from the beginning.

At government counters, we still occasionally hear familiar lines: "Server is down," "Come tomorrow," "Missing one document," or the classic "System not working."

Change is here, but it is uneven, scattered, learning its way forward.

Still, there is hope.
Hope that systems will become smoother.
Hope that access will become equal.
Hope that the simplicity that cities experience will eventually reach every small town and every remote village.

One day, perhaps, the transition from physical files to digital portals will feel complete not just technologically, but experientially.

And maybe, when that day comes, we will finally live in a world where the chaos of paperwork is only a memory, the queues are rare, and everyone regardless of where they live can navigate life not with stress, but with confidence.

Chapter 11: From Shops to Online Shopping

There was a time when shopping meant stepping out only, feeling the texture of things, bargaining with shopkeepers, and carrying bags home.

Before online shopping, every purchase was a small adventure. Kids in the house were often the ones sent to corner stores to buy small, essential items like sugar, biscuits, milk, or snacks.

Walking there meant seeing familiar faces, greeting neighbours, and sometimes running into friends along the way. Every trip was a small responsibility, a lesson in independence and awareness of the world outside the home.
Sometimes, kids get sent to the corner store multiple times a day, especially when guests arrive.

As children, we were often given a little pocket money when sent to the shop. After buying the required sugar, milk, or biscuits, we used the leftover coins to secretly reward ourselves with chocolates or anything that comes with it. Those errands taught us small lessons, how to manage change, make choices, and experience the tiny thrill of earning a treat.

Back then, shopping taught us more than just buying. In the process, children learn not only to remember household items but also to keep track of what's spent. It taught them patience, waiting in queues, walking in the afternoon heat, or saving pocket money until we could buy something we wanted. It taught the decision-making like choosing between two flavours, two colours, or two brands without endless reviews. It taught us communication asking the shopkeeper for the freshest packet, explaining what we needed, or learning how to politely ask for a small discount. It also taught us responsibility, carrying everything home without dropping anything on the way.

For adults, walking to local markets, street bazaars and department stores shaped their routines. Interactions with shopkeepers were personal. They remembered our preferences, recommended products, and sometimes even offered small discounts because they knew us. We often carried cash, calculating change, and relished the process of selecting each item carefully.

From negotiating prices for toys to bargaining over vegetables, every transaction was an exchange, not just of money, but of smiles, patience, and human connection.

Then came catalogues, phone orders, and early e-commerce websites. We hesitated, unsure if items would match their photos or arrive on time. The first online purchase was both thrilling and nerve-wracking. A toy, a book, or a gadget ordered with excitement and anticipation.

Slow delivery times, incorrect shipments, and the need to track orders manually taught patience. But gradually, we embraced online shopping. Convenience outweighed uncertainty. Credit cards, net banking, and COD options made transactions easier. E-commerce giants emerged, offering variety that no single store could match.

Today, online shopping is seamless. Everything from groceries and clothes to electronics and luxury items is just a tap away. Delivery apps, express shipping, and customer reviews make shopping faster and more informed. We could browse hundreds of products in minutes, compare prices instantly, and avoid crowded markets or long queues. Shopping became efficient, predictable, and effortless.

And now, anything manufactured in any small corner of the country, a handmade terracotta lamp from a village in Bengal, a pickle from Guntur, a handwoven stole from Kutch, anything can be ordered and delivered to our doorstep. Artisans who once relied on weekly bazaars or word-of-mouth now have storefronts on global marketplaces. Their products travel farther than they ever could. In a strange way, geography shrank, and access expanded.

Today's children are adding things into digital carts. They don't wait, and they rarely walk to nearby stores especially in cities. If their favourite kids' toothpaste isn't at home, they don't want to adjust with what's available. Instead, they say, "Order it in Blinkit and let it come," expecting it instantly, the way they expect everything else. Their world is built on speed: quick searches, instant delivery, no waiting, no walking, no bargaining.

Shopping has become quiet and isolated. The phone does the talking, the app does the choosing, and the delivery partner does the carrying. Children no longer know the warmth of being recognised at the local store or the pride of coming home with exactly what was asked for. They know speed, accuracy, and efficiency skills of a different world.

While traditional shopping still exists, much of its personal touch has been lost to the ease of online shopping especially in cities.

We used to carry heavy 10 kg rice bags ourselves, feeling the weight in our hands and the effort in each step. Today, they're delivered to our doorstep, along with almost everything else. The physical effort, the small routines, and even the little triumphs of carrying home what we bought all have been replaced by convenience.

Sometimes I wonder if we miss the little joys of old shopping trips: chatting with shopkeepers, discovering new corners of the market, or carefully selecting items. Even the minor inconveniences like waiting for change, hunting for the ripest fruit, or negotiating a discount added texture to life.

Growing up in both worlds, we learned to appreciate both the charm of human interaction and the efficiency of digital convenience.

Nostalgia still lingers—not as resistance to change, but as a reminder of where we came from. The markets of our childhood weren't just places to buy things; they were small theatres of life. There were arguments over price, accidental discoveries, familiar vendors, and that simple joy of carrying something home wrapped in newspaper, as if it were treasure.

The grocery list that doesn't crumble in our hands or pockets, it sits neatly inside an app. Yet strangely, even with all this convenience, those old memories never faded. They sit quietly at the back of the mind, surfacing at odd moments like when the delivery guy rings the bell, or when a parcel arrives wrapped in too much packaging, reminding us of a time when purchases came with less cardboard and more conversation.

Perhaps that's our generation's quiet superpower: we can move fluently between two worlds without rejecting either.

We can smile at the chaos of a crowded market and still appreciate the silent precision of a one-click order.
We know what it means to wait—really wait—yet we also know the thrill of delivery in minutes.

We understand the value of time saved, yet we hold a soft corner for the time spent wandering through aisles.

Maybe that's what makes our generation unique. These dual experiences shaped us not just as consumers, but as individuals capable of valuing both patience and efficiency, human connection and digital convenience and to make the best use of it.

We remember a time before "Add to Cart."
And living between these two worlds -
the one that required footsteps, and
the one that now requires just fingertips.

Chapter 12: From Ticket Counters to Online Booking

There was a time when getting a ticket whether for a movie, a bus, a train, or even a special event meant more than just securing a seat. It meant stepping out with a plan, preparing for a queue, and carrying some cash neatly tucked inside. The journey began much before the actual journey. We left home early, hoping the line wouldn't be too long, and mentally prepared ourself for the possibility of returning without the ticket we wanted. But that, too, was part of the experience and it was normal.

For Movie tickets, we reached the theatre much before the showtime, walked toward the counter where people were already crowding around, and stood in a line that moved slowly, one person at a time. The big boards displayed the movie names in bold letters, with showtimes written beside them, and a red "Housefull" board hanging somewhere at the corner. Everyone feared that board. The uncertainty added a strange thrill. We could be the next one in line, and suddenly the board would come down with a thud - show full/ Housefull. We might feel disappointed, but also felt alive in that moment, because we were part of a shared human experience.

There were no previews of seat layouts, no guarantee of getting the perfect row, and definitely no way to book seats weeks in advance. The excitement began from the counter itself. When we finally reached the front, the clerk barely looked up. "How many?" he would ask, his fingers already on the stamping machine. "Two balconies", hoping balcony wasn't sold out. If we were lucky, we got what we wanted. If not, we settled for whatever remained whether the first class, second class, or even the front rows where we had to crane our neck upward to watch the screen. But nobody complained too much. We just adjusted, because that's how life worked then. Adjustment was a habit we didn't even question.

Bus and train tickets had their own ticket booking counters. For trains especially, the queue started before sunrise on some days. Everyone in the queue knew each other by the end of the wait. We shared snacks, exchanged travel tips, and sometimes even held someone's place in line when they needed to step away for a minute. When the reservation charts came out, people huddled around them, running their fingers down the printed lists looking for their names. Getting a confirmed seat was a small achievement in itself. We celebrated it the way we now celebrate express delivery.

Bus tickets for long-distance journeys were handwritten at the counters. The person behind the desk used a duplicate slip book with carbon paper in between. He wrote our name, the seat number, and the date, and tore off a thin paper strip for us. That strip felt like a promise, a promise that the next morning, we would be on our way. And that was enough.

Getting the seats in the same row for the family members was challenging and we requested the co-passengers for exchange.

In those days, the value of the ticket wasn't just the paper. It was the entire process, the waiting, the uncertainty, and the patience. We didn't just click and confirm. We earned it.

And somewhere in that phase of paper tickets, there was another universal experience, the brief heart attack of misplacing them.

Every ticket, whether it was for a movie or a train, suddenly became the most important thing once we had it in hand. We tucked it carefully into wallets, shirt pockets, purses, books or sometimes even inside the watch strap. And yet, just before the entry point - we always checked again.

Once.
Twice.
Sometimes three times.

That tiny moment between thinking **"I kept it here..."** and finally finding it sitting neatly where we left it, felt like an emotional roller coaster.

Then came a period of slow change. Landline phones became more common, and some theatres allowed phone reservations. We could call, request a seat, and pick up the ticket an hour before the show. It felt magical at that time. Similarly, travel agents began booking bus and train tickets for us. We paid them a small service fee, and they stood in the queue on our behalf. Suddenly, the system felt more convenient. We didn't have to wake up early or stand under the sun. Someone else did it for us.

Then came the real revolution, the arrival of computers and early internet. Websites appeared where we could check train availability. It still did not allow booking in the beginning, but just seeing seat status online felt unbelievable. We refreshed the page repeatedly, checking if seats had moved from "Waiting List 25" to "Waiting List 24." That was considered progress.

The first-time people booked a ticket online, it felt like a gamble.
What if the transaction failed?
What if the seat wasn't confirmed?
What if the page froze?
We held our breath until the small confirmation message appeared. A simple PDF ticket felt like a miracle no paper slip, no manual entries, no queue.

As online booking platforms developed, life changed. We could now choose our seat, compare prices, view seat maps, filter by date, time, preference, or even the side of the bus we wanted to sit on. Payment options grew, debit cards, credit cards, net banking, wallets, UPI. Everything became safe, fast, predictable.

Booking a movie ticket online was a big milestone for many. Choosing our favourite row, paying instantly, and walking directly into the theatre without waiting at the counter felt like stepping into the future. Soon, QR codes replaced printed tickets. Even the physical ticket collectors disappeared; scanners took their place.

Travel became even easier. Today, we book entire holidays within minutes. Flights, trains, buses, hotels all done without stepping outside. We know seat positions, food options, arrival timings, and the entire experience before even beginning the journey. Booking, cancelling, modifying and everything is effortless.

Convenience again won.

The nervousness of watching the reservation chart being put up… forgotten.
The feeling of holding a thin paper ticket carefully so it didn't tear… disappeared.
The shared frustration and shared excitement with strangers in queues… replaced by silent scrolling.

Sometimes I think about children growing up today. They don't know the feeling of standing in line, counting the people before them, hoping the tickets won't run out.

If their favourite movie is not available in the nearest theatre, they simply check another one. If a bus seat isn't available, they check another app. If they don't get the exact seat they want, they wait for one more refresh. They expect the world to match their preference instantly. Even tickets are no longer something they "go and get." They add to cart, scan, and move on.

Their world is efficient — ours was experiential.
Their world is accurate — ours was unpredictable.
Their world delivers — ours demanded effort.

Neither is wrong. Just different.

In contrast, we grew up learning patience, not because we tried to learn it, but because life taught it naturally. We stood in lines, accepted what was available, made the best of it, and found joy in the process.

Today's generation is growing up with choice, speed, and precision. Everything is predictable. Everything is customisable. Everything is available at the tap of a finger.

And that's okay. That's their world.

We remember the ticket counters.
We remember the long lines.
We remember the little slips of paper that held huge meaning.
We remember the worry of losing them and the relief of finding them.
We remember uncertainty and excitement living side by side.

Today, a small QR code on a glowing screen holds everything, the seat, the timing, the journey.

Maybe that's what makes our generation unique.
We lived through both worlds, the world of standing in lines and the world of instant booking.
The world of handwritten slips and the world of digital confirmations.

We also navigate mobile apps like second nature. We know the value of time, but we also know the value of waiting.

Our memories stand somewhere in between queues and QR codes.

And perhaps that's our quiet advantage that we carry two worlds with us. And that's why, even today, when we book a ticket online, there's a small part of us that remembers how it once felt to stand at a counter, count the people ahead, and hope the stamp wouldn't say "Housefull."

A small part of us still smiles at those memories not because we want them back, but because they shaped who we are.

We remember a time before "Confirm Booking". And that old memories sit inside us like an untorn ticket - still valid, still precious, still ours.

Chapter 13: From Auto Stands to Algorithmic Rides

There was a time when traveling meant stepping out of the house, walking to the auto stand, and hoping that the day's luck was kind. The auto stand was not just a place; it was an experience. It carried a mini-culture of its own. The cluster of parked autos lined imperfectly, the drivers gathered in small groups discussing everything from politics to last night's cricket match, and the familiar rhythm of negotiations that began the moment we approached.

Before apps, we didn't need notifications. We heard one specific horn tone and immediately knew: "an auto is free..."

Sometimes they slowed down beside us and gave that subtle half-head-nod, the universal sign for **"Going? Tell me your destination."**

It was an interaction built on human judgment, instinct, and unspoken rules. Some days we got a polite driver who agreed instantly. Some days we walked away after the classic "Meter?" debate. And yet, for many of us, these were normal, even comforting, parts of everyday life. If we found an auto during monsoon, it wasn't a ride, it was a rescue mission.

If it was festival season, exam time, or Friday evening:
Fare doubled. No explanation needed.

The final five minutes of every ride were not about reaching the destination, but about searching for change.

The driver checked his little metal tray.
We checked every pocket including the secret zip in the wallet.

Many friendships were built over:
"I'll give you □2 next time."

As cities expanded and commutes stretched, auto stands became the small anchors of predictability. We knew exactly which corner to find them, which drivers were usually willing to go our side, and which ones would say no even before we finished our sentence. These were not perfect systems, but they were rooted in familiarity. There were frustrations, yes, but also a sense of shared understanding two humans trying to match time, need, distance, and convenience.

What began as simple GPS maps soon grew into full-fledged ride-hailing ecosystems. Before we knew it, "I'll go get an auto" became "I'll book a ride." The transformation was not sudden, yet when we look back, it feels like we switched eras in a matter of days. From standing under the sun and waiting uncertainly, we moved to tapping a screen and watching a tiny animated car approach us with algorithmic precision. The physical auto stand dissolved into an invisible network distributed across the city, every street, every building, every lane became a potential pick-up point.

The biggest shift was not in the rides themselves, but in the mindset. Earlier, travel depended on people, drivers who knew the shortcuts, recognized regular passengers, and were part of the everyday reality of the neighbourhood. Today, travel depends on systems, apps that calculate demand, prices that change by the minute, and routes that are optimized not by experience but by real-time data. We went from reading the expressions of a driver to reading digital ratings.

Convenience became the new currency. No more searching for change, no more bargaining, no more waiting under the heat. The app brought structure, predictability, and accountability. It even brought something unthinkable in the old days, transparency. We could see the fare upfront, the route mapped clearly, the driver's credentials, and an entire journey logged second-by-second. Safety features multiplied. Digital payments replaced pockets filled with coins. Life got smoother, faster, more automated.

Yet with every gain, something quiet slipped away.

The small human interactions reduced. The casual greetings, the familiar faces at the auto stand, the rhythm of spontaneous conversations, all scattered into digital silence. Today, we enter a ride, check the driver's name for verification, and then look at our phones until we reach. Transportation is now less about travel and more about transitioning from one task to another. The journey has become the pause between two activities rather than an experience in itself.

The algorithm brought efficiency, but it also brought distance. The driver is no longer someone from our neighbourhood; he might be from a different corner of the city, connected only through the app. The conversations are fewer because the metrics matter more. Ratings influence behaviour, not natural interaction. Both sides know they are being evaluated, so the engagement becomes polite, filtered, and cautious. What was once a simple ride is now part of a larger digital ecosystem governed by data.

Even the unpredictability has changed shape. Earlier, the uncertainty was human, will I get an auto? Will he agree? Will the fare be reasonable? Now the unpredictability is technical will there be surge pricing? Will the app match a nearby driver or someone 12 minutes away? Will the map take the right route or lead us into unnecessary loops? The challenges remain, only their faces have changed.

The emotional shift is subtle but significant. In the old days, we felt connected to the rhythm of our locality. The auto stand was part of the community landscape. We knew the familiar morning bustle. We knew where the rush hours peaked. We knew when the drivers took their chai break. This familiarity added warmth to everyday routines.

Today, the experience is universal but impersonal. The app works the same way in every city, every state, every country. The ride experience could feel identical whether we are in Bengaluru, or Mumbai. That standardization has brought comfort.

And yet, this evolution also reflects who we have become. Life today is faster, more structured, more multitasked. We optimize everything from time, effort, cost, convenience. In such a world, the old system of waiting at an auto stand feels like a luxury we no longer have patience for. We prioritize efficiency, even if it costs us some human warmth. We prefer the precision of systems over the unpredictability of people because our schedules no longer accommodate the chaos of manual commuting.

Growing up between this shift from auto stands to algorithmic rides, mirrors the larger story of our times. We moved from unstructured life to system-driven living, from the warmth of personal interactions to the quiet precision of technologically managed efficiency. What once depended on familiarity, negotiation, and shared local culture has now become a set of buttons, prompts, and predictable processes.

The journey that earlier began with a conversation, a smile, or even a small argument now starts with a screen tap. And as we transitioned from community-based routines to individually personalized routes, we didn't just change how we travel, we changed how we live, how we connect, and how we understand the world around us.

Earlier, we ended rides with a quick nod, a half-smile, sometimes a blessing, or sometimes irritation, but always **human acknowledgment** and not a 5-star rating and reviews.

Yet, there is something resilient about memories. Even today, when we pass an auto stand in certain places, it brings a faint smile. It reminds us of simpler mornings, impatient school runs, office-day bargaining, and small but meaningful interactions. It reminds us that not everything needs to be perfect to be memorable. Sometimes the imperfections leave deeper imprints than the polished convenience of modern systems.

The future will continue evolving. Autonomous vehicles, AI-driven route optimization, subscription-based mobility, and even driverless pods may soon become part of everyday life.

The idea of waiting at a stand might feel like a chapter from a distant past. But the emotional memory of that era, the human messiness, the spontaneity, the everyday negotiations, the familiar faces will remain one of the soft, warm corners of urban nostalgia.

Because between the old auto stands and the new algorithmic rides lies the story of us, our habits, our priorities, our changing pace of life. The technology reshapes how we move, how we interact, and how we experience the world around us.

We remember a time before "Book My Ride".
A time when rides weren't summoned by GPS,
but by eye contact, a raised hand, and a shared
understanding of direction, distance, and humanity.

Chapter 14: From Floor trading to Online trading

The market once lived in motion and sound. Voices shouted prices, hands signalled deals, and papers rustled in urgent rhythm. Every transaction carried tension, every tick of the ticker felt like a heartbeat. The trading floor was chaos and order intertwined alive, unpredictable, and deeply human.

Each gesture, glance, and pause had meaning. Patience, instinct, observation, and courage shaped outcomes, while impulsiveness demanded an immediate price. Traders often placed orders simply because someone else did, bias born from proximity rather than reasoning.

Back then, the stock market wasn't for everyone. It was a space reserved for those genuinely interested and those willing to engage fully. Participation required presence, discipline, courage, and confidence. Information was scarce, learning came through experience, and progress demanded repeated exposure to uncertainty. The energy of the floor was intense and exclusive understood only by those inside it.

Trading required attention to details, an untrained eye would never notice. Portfolios were maintained in notebooks and loose papers, and trade confirmations arrived only after days or sometimes weeks. Investors relied entirely on physical interaction or telephone calls to place buy or sell orders with their brokers. Every transaction required contact, and with prices changing by the minute, even a small delay could cost significantly.

Only a few people traded full-time. For most, the process felt complicated, intimidating, and risky. With limited transparency and slow access to information, many viewed stocks trading not as investing, but as a gamble, unpredictable and unsafe.

Because participation was low, the number of listed companies remained limited, and liquidity in the market stayed low. Earlier, trading decisions were driven mostly by fundamentals, company value, financial strength, management quality, and long-term potential. And, for most people, the market felt distant, only a few understood or dared to approach.

Traders moved weaving through the flow of energy around them. Every shout, every hand signal, every nod carried meaning. It was instinct, experience, and quick judgment combined. Each decision could tip the balance between gain and loss. Success was measured in persistence, focus, and subtlety; failure was immediate, sometimes public, and deeply instructive.

The floor was alive. The tension was palpable. Papers were crumpled in frustration, fingers scribbled numbers with lightning speed, and voices competed with one another in a symphony of urgency. Patterns emerged from noise, opportunities hid in movement, and discipline was constantly tested. Traders learned to anticipate, to trust intuition, to read the unspoken signals that decided fortunes in seconds.

Every trade was a lesson in observation. It taught the patience to wait for the right moment, the ability to act decisively under pressure, and the skill to navigate complexity while remaining composed. The market did not forgive error easily. Impulsive decisions were costly. Repetition and careful attention, built mastery.

In this world, failure was not a setback but a teacher. Losing a trade, misreading a gesture, or missing a signal provided lessons that no book could convey. The market demanded engagement, presence, and continuous learning.
It was unforgiving, thrilling, and entirely human.

But, with the arrival of computers and internet, an entire ecosystem has emerged. Then the floor began to vanish. The tangible energy of people moving, papers rustling, and voices overlapping transformed into a quiet hum of notifications, charts, and blinking numbers. The chaos became invisible.

Patience and observation remained crucial, but the challenges became new: the flood of information, the speed of decision-making, and the quiet pressure of acting in a space that felt vast, fast, and impersonal. The medium changed, but the principles endured. Observation, discipline, and courage continued to shape success.

The shift reflected more than technological progress. Online trading demands adaptation. Attention shifts from gestures to charts, from instinct to analysis. Success depends on strategy, focus, and the ability to respond calmly to fast-moving information. The rhythm was hidden in data, not gestures. The market evolved from a physical theatre to a digital arena.

Online trading made access easier, but the market remained a world of rules, strategy, and skill. Then came the apps. Mobile platforms brought trading to pockets, fingertips, and living rooms. Suddenly, the stock market was not a distant world for a few professionals; it became visible, accessible, and approachable for everyone. Notifications, tutorials, instant updates, and easy interfaces opened trading to millions. Awareness grew. Conversations about investments became common. No longer a secret club, the market became part of everyday life.

Numerous tools, platforms, and apps assist investors in research, execution, and predictions. Companies now exist solely to educate, guide portfolios, and support financial planning. Screens replaced shouting, algorithms replaced instinct, and trades happened in milliseconds with clicks and taps.

Everything has changed. Today, alongside fundamentals, traders rely on technical indicators, candlestick patterns, data analytics, and complex studies that interpret market behaviour in real time.

The language of the market itself has expanded. Derivatives, leverage, pledging, margin trading, options strategies, futures, and hedging have become everyday terms for many investors. Yet, in the earlier era, the market was far simpler. Most dealt only with equities, and even that felt overwhelming. Stocks were considered risky, not because they lacked strength, but because awareness, access, and financial literacy were limited.

Now, almost everyone's savings—directly or indirectly—flow into the markets through mutual funds, SIPs, ETFs, or personal portfolios.

And then came algorithmic trading, for experts fluent in data, systems, and strategy. The High-frequency trading, shifting the role of the trader from participant to architect. Machines executing trades in microseconds, faster than any human could process. Algorithms followed rules, scanned patterns, and reacted instantly to price movements. What once required observation and human intuition now required understanding systems, coding logic, and trusting machines to execute strategy flawlessly.

Algorithmic trading added new lessons. Speed and accuracy became paramount. Emotions were removed from execution. The human challenge shifted from acting to designing systems that act. Patience became not about waiting in the crowd but about programming the right conditions, monitoring results, and adjusting strategy. The rhythm of the market was still present, but it moved in ways invisible to the naked eye, measurable only in microseconds and algorithmic performance.

The world of investments has expanded far beyond the stock market floors of the past. Stocks, once a domain for a few who studied charts, attended floors, or followed brokers closely, are now just one part of a broader spectrum. Mutual funds allow people to invest collectively, spreading risk while still participating in growth.

Awareness has grown alongside accessibility. Financial literacy campaigns, investment apps, and online platforms have made information available to anyone willing to look. Discussions about asset allocation, risk management, and long-term planning are no longer limited to professionals, they are part of everyday conversations. Even small investors can track performance, understand diversification, and explore a variety of options that were once hidden behind complex jargon.

This democratization of investment has shifted the market from a selective space to one that welcomes participation from anyone curious or committed. The tools are different, but the principles remain: understanding risk, making informed choices, and exercising patience.

While access has widened, the discipline required to navigate investments successfully continues to be essential. Knowledge, awareness, and careful planning have become as important as capital in ensuring growth and stability.

Machines could execute trades, but humans still had to anticipate patterns, define strategy, and learn from outcomes. Algorithmic trading reflected life in a new way: complexity increased, speed accelerated, and precision became critical, but the underlying human qualities, observation, patience, courage, adaptability, remained central.

Both methods offer lessons in navigation, control, and foresight. Floor trading taught presence and intuition. Online trading teaches precision and analytical thinking. Together, they reveal the timeless human need to adapt, observe, and act wisely. Both are arenas where skill meets uncertainty, where learning is continuous, and where mastery is earned.

The medium may evolve, the game may become faster, and the noise may disappear, but the essence - the challenge, the lesson, the growth remains unchanged.

The market, in every form, continues to teach the same truths. Preparation matters. Impulsiveness is costly. Learning is continuous. Success is temporary, and humility is essential.

From the chaotic energy of the floor to the quiet precision of online platforms, the rhythm persists: notice, act, learn, repeat. The tools change, but the lessons endure—timeless, subtle, and human.

Trading may have evolved into high-speed, data-driven precision, but at its core, it still reflects the age-old balance between risk and reward, echoing an era before "Make money by investing in stock markets" became a marketing script.

Chapter 15: From Encyclopaedias to AI Prompts

There was a time when learning meant flipping pages, hunting for meaning, and sitting with thick books that felt heavier than our school bags. Before the internet and AI became a regular visitor in our homes, knowledge lived inside books. Real books. Heavy, textured, printed books with pages that smelled like a mixt of ink, dust and time.

Every home had at least one English dictionary - the Oxford dictionary or the English to Local language dictionary, sizes vary from small(pocket) to big. Some houses had encyclopaedias, those grand, multi-volume treasures that made a home look instantly "educated."

Opening them wasn't casual; it was a small ceremony. We sat down, placed them on the table, and slowly flipped through thin pages because one wrong move could tear them. If we wanted to know the meaning of photosynthesis, we didn't tap. We **searched**, alphabet by alphabet, with patience. Sometimes, we got sidetracked seeing other words along the way, words we never planned to learn. The learning was accidental, natural, and often slow.

Even brands understood the value these books carried. Some products like Milo came with free dictionaries, small world atlases, or fact books for children. Those were treasures, small, colourful, filled with maps, flags, capitals, amazing facts, and pictures so fascinating that kids would keep them safe like secret possessions. They weren't just product add-ons; they were doors to a bigger world, especially for households that couldn't afford expensive encyclopaedias.

For school projects, we depended on library hours, borrowing reference books, and handwritten notes passed down from seniors and friends. School projects meant sitting with books spread across the table, sketch pens lying around, newspapers cut and saved for reference. We had to read, underline, write in our own words, and sometimes even draw diagrams manually. There were no shortcuts. The more time we spent, the more we absorbed.

Library periods were not just about reading; they were about waiting for our turn to borrow books. Some books were always unavailable, always issued out to someone else. That scarcity made learning feel valuable. We waited, and waiting made knowledge feel earned.

We remember the librarian stamping books with a heavy thud, the return date circled in thick red ink, a reminder that learning had timelines, and responsibility was part of it.

When teachers gave meanings as homework, we read, compared, and wrote them manually. Correcting spelling mistakes meant rewriting entire pages. For essays, we collected points from magazines, newspapers, and reference books like Rank scorer etc. For GK exams, we read fact books until they became soft at the corners. Dictionaries and encyclopaedias shaped not just our knowledge but our patience, discipline, and curiosity.

The Encyclopaedias were not just sources of information; they were symbols. If a home had one, it meant learning was taken seriously. Parents bought them during exhibitions. Salesmen came home with one sample volume and convinced families to buy the entire set on instalment. We, as children, opened them more out of fascination than necessity. The glossy pictures, world maps, diagrams of planets, charts of animals each page felt like a new world.

Turning the pages of dictionaries, atlases, and encyclopaedias taught us discipline. Every time we opened a book, we opened a small window into the world outside our home. Whether it was learning the capital of Kenya, the meaning of "empathy," or locating the Amazon River on a map, knowledge felt like a discovery.

And tucked between all of this was a beautiful truth: We were learning without realising we were learning.

But there was also a tiny fear:
Don't tear the page.
Don't underline.
Don't fold the corners.
Don't touch with dirty hands.

Books demanded discipline.

Dictionaries taught rules even before they taught meanings.

Then came the early internet era, the first crack in the encyclopaedia's kingdom.

Typing a question into a search box felt strange. We weren't used to receiving answers instantly, Pages loaded line by line, and we watched pixels appear slowly. Search engines were new, unfamiliar, and not always accurate. Still, they felt magical. Suddenly definitions, facts, images and answers arrived without flipping any pages.

Slowly, dictionaries turned into websites. Encyclopaedias turned into Wikipedia. The habit of flipping pages began to fade.

Today, we type a few words, hit enter, and answers arrive instantly neat, organised, and served to us in seconds.

Why search for ten minutes when the answer came in two seconds?

Students started printing material from the internet. Teachers began accepting online references. Dictionaries and encyclopaedias remained at home, but they were no longer touched as often. They began gathering dust, and no one noticed.

We still used books for school projects, but the initial outline came from the internet. The internet became the new teacher, but it wasn't yet smart. It gave what we asked, not what we needed. It lacked depth, understanding, and human-like explanation. Still, it marked the beginning of a shift, a shift from page numbers to search bars, from indexes to keywords, from manual effort to digital shortcuts.

Then came smartphones, and with them, the speed of learning changed forever.

Dictionaries became apps.
Encyclopaedias became interactive.
Atlases became zoomable maps with street views, satellite images, and 3D visuals.

If search engines gave answers, AI began giving explanations.

AI did not just show information; it processed it, organised it, rewrote it, simplified it, expanded it, and personalised it. It became a study partner, a writing companion, a homework helper, and sometimes even an emotional support system. With AI, we did not learn alone; we learned together.

Today, knowledge feels alive.

We no longer search using keywords; we **talk**.

We ask:

"Explain this in simple words."
"Write a summary."
"Give me examples."
"How do I do this?"
"Rewrite this better."
"Create a story about this topic."
"Help me understand."

AI doesn't just answer questions; it understands intention. It gives us the answer we meant to ask. It remembers patterns, adapts to style, and gives personalised explanations, something books could never do.

Dictionaries taught us meanings.
Encyclopaedias taught us facts.
Search engines taught us speed.

But AI?
AI teaches us possibility.

Today's children don't flip dictionaries.
They don't underline text.
They don't copy definitions into notebooks 10 times each.

They open a device and type:

"Explain in easy words."

And the answer appears instantly.

Earlier, a student preparing for exams had stacks of books around them. Now, they sit with tabs and apps open. Earlier, confusion meant asking a teacher or parent. Now it means typing a question in AI.

Learning has changed shape.
The weight of books is gone.
The weight of thinking has also reduced.

But learning hasn't become lesser. It has just become faster.

The biggest gift AI gave us is clarity with speed.
Explanations are simpler.
Examples are better.
Understanding is cleaner.
And time is saved, allowing deeper learning or faster decision-making.

AI also makes creativity accessible: poem writing, story making, brainstorming ideas, generating explanations, simplifying difficult concepts. One request is all it takes.

Even adults, who once searched pages for meanings, now ask AI to write emails, prepare summaries, or help with decisions. Knowledge, once slow and effortful, is now flowing like water easy to access, ready to use.

Knowledge once required effort.
Today, it requires intention.

Earlier, books forced us to think slowly.
AI helps us move quickly.
Both have value.
Both shaped us.

Growing up between the two worlds, we know the weight of a dictionary and the power of a prompt. We know how it feels to search manually and how it feels to get instant answers. And now we see children asking AI for homework help.

From bulky dictionaries and encyclopaedias to intelligent AI prompts, the way we seek knowledge has transformed completely. And somewhere in that journey, we grew up experiencing both the slow search and the instant response.

We have lived through the three, the slow world of flipping pages, the medium world of Google searches and the fast world of AI explanations.

And because we lived all three, our understanding is richer.

We know the importance of effort.
We also know the convenience of shortcuts.
We know how humans teach.
We also know how machines guide.

Today, prompts are the new index.
They are our way of navigating knowledge.

Instead of:

"Find the page."
"Check the index."
"Search alphabetically."

We now say:

"Explain like I'm a beginner."
"Give real examples and explain."

Sometimes when we see dictionaries untouched in shelves or encyclopaedias stored in boxes, we feel a quiet nostalgia. Those books were part of our childhood, our projects, our exams, our slow afternoons. They taught us persistence.

Yet, there is beauty in what we have today too. AI encourages curiosity. It makes learning accessible to anyone, anywhere. A child who once feared asking questions now asks AI without hesitation. Knowledge is no longer limited by books or geography.

We may have lost the romance of slow learning, but we gained the courage to explore far more than we ever could.

Knowledge has become lighter, but imagination has become larger.

From heavy encyclopaedias to lightweight prompts, our journey reflects how learning itself transformed:

From effort to efficiency.
From memorising to understanding.
From searching alone to learning with support.
From waiting for answers to receiving them instantly.

We stand at the centre of this evolution, carrying both worlds with us. We remember dictionaries being passed from hand to hand, and today, we pass prompts from mind to machine. We learnt discipline from books and possibilities from AI. Both left their mark on us.

Maybe that's what makes our generation special.

We are not just readers.
We are not just searchers.
We are prompt thinkers,
We survived the slow world, embraced the fast world, and learned to blend both with grace.

And somewhere between flipping pages and typing questions, we didn't just learn new things but we learned new ways of learning.

We remember a time before ChatGPT, Gemini, Copilot, and Perplexity -
before screens became classrooms,
and prompts replaced page numbers.
A time when we trusted books, teachers, and our

own effort
more than any algorithm.

Once, we memorised spellings from dictionaries.
Today, autocorrect shakes its head and fixes them for us.
And in that journey—from paper to prompt—lies the story of our generation.

Chapter 16: From Casual Lessons to Coaching class

There was a time when learning came quietly soft, unannounced, and woven into everyday life. The home, the veranda, the street, and even the small gaps between daily chores used to be our classrooms. Lessons unfolded without anyone announcing that a "class has begun." We absorbed things because they surrounded us. They belonged to us. They were passed down without certificates, yet they shaped us for life.

Growing up, almost everything we learned happened through observation, participation, and repetition. No one "taught" us how to draw a rangoli, for example. We watched our mother or grandmother bend over the ground at dawn, rice flour slipping between their fingers like a rhythm older than memory. The curves, the dots, the symmetry, none of it felt like a subject. It was simply a movement we grew into. One morning, we just found ourself kneeling beside them, imitating the motion, failing, trying again, and eventually getting it right. No one corrected us with a red pen. No one asked us to join a weekend workshop on "Rangoli for Beginners." It was a life skill passed from one generation to the next without fanfare.

In our school days, almost every south Indian girl had a rangoli or kolam book. Especially in South

India, where rangoli wasn't just decoration but a daily ritual, an offering, a welcome, a rhythm of dawn. On the way to and from school, we would slow down as we passed houses, not because we were curious about the people living inside, but because we wanted to see the rangoli patterns drawn in front of their homes. The designs changed with seasons, festivals, and moods. Some patterns had straight lines, some had flowing curves, and some used dots that formed intricate shapes once the lines connected them.

We memorized those patterns silently, as if they were a secret message meant only for those paying attention. And as soon as we reached school or sometimes even in the corridor before assembly, we opened our notebooks and tried capturing what we had seen. There were days when the design slipped halfway from memory, leaving us stuck, staring at half-finished dots. So, we invented the missing parts. Maybe the curves weren't exact, the symmetry was off, or the pattern looked slightly different, but that never bothered us. Imperfection wasn't failure, it was creativity.

We shared our notebooks like treasures. "This one I drew from Shanthi Akka's house." "This one came from a festival competition." "This one I copied from my school friend Sudha." There was pride in knowing a rare pattern. There was joy in exchanging new ones. It wasn't just drawing; it was social learning long before the term existed.

During festivals, the excitement doubled. Every house seemed to try something extraordinary. Competitions were held in temples, schools, and community centres. We selected the most elaborate designs, practiced them during weekends, and sometimes even woke up earlier than usual to perfect the final version. The pages of our rangoli books carried faint pencil marks, erased attempts, smudges of colour, and sometimes tiny notes: "12 dots to 6, straight pattern". Those books weren't just notebooks; they were personal museums.

Some designs came from magazines. During summer vacations, we share the fortnightly magazines like **Vikatan** and **Rani**. Inside, tucked between stories and recipes, were two or three pages dedicated to kolam patterns. We tore those pages out carefully or copied the designs into rough paper and later transferred them neatly into our books. Each design had a story, a location, a memory. Even today, we can recall which pattern came from which place or person.

Looking back, we now understand that these weren't just childhood pastimes. Without realizing, we were learning proportion, symmetry, spatial memory, design thinking, patience, and persistence, skills that today are taught in structured art classes or design workshops.

Cooking was another silent lesson. They learned while standing beside someone older. The heat of the stove, the whistle of the pressure cooker, the smell of tempering, all of these were the teachers. By the time we grew up, we could make tea without being "taught." We could chop vegetables by copying the steady movements we had seen for years. We knew how much salt to add not because we had measured it with a spoon but because our eyes had trained themselves to see "just enough."

Even things like sewing a button, folding clothes neatly, organizing the kitchen shelves, identifying which spice goes with which recipe, understanding how to store vegetables so they last longer, these were not part of a curriculum. These were part of life. Some skills were intentional; others were accidental. But they all came naturally.

And drawing cartoons? It came from Boomer cards taped to steel cupboards, from comic strips in newspapers, and from trying—over and over—to perfect Mickey Mouse ears or the curve of a favourite character's smile. The first victory wasn't applause; it was when a friend said, "Hey, that looks like the original!"

Children once learned gardening simply by watching elders tend to plants. They learned how to reuse, repair, and adjust things without being told they were practicing "sustainability." Children learned how to ride a bicycle from older cousins holding the seat from behind. Some picked up crochet patterns sitting in the evening light with aunties who never called it a "class." Everything was one long, seamless process of living and learning.

But somewhere, as time moved ahead, the world shifted. The value of learning became closely tied to formal instruction. Today, everything has a class. Everything has a fee. Everything needs a registration link or a Zoom ID. The casual lessons we absorbed by just being part of a home now arrive in the form of coaching centres, weekend workshops, specialized tutors, or online courses.

The transition from casual lessons to a full-fledged coaching culture has also changed how we perceive learning. Earlier, learning was a natural by-product of living. It happened as we observed, tried, failed, and tried again. Now, we feel to master every skill; being "good enough" is no longer enough. Learning has become like a scheduled task, something we must plan, enrol for, and pay for. Skill-building has become an industry, and knowledge is marketed like a commodity.

Classical dance, which children once learned from the neighbourhood teacher who charged very little and taught with devotion, is now offered through glossy studios with package deals and annual shows. Even hobbies like drawing or music, once enjoyed casually, now became a structured curriculum.

This shift has positives. There is beauty in what formal learning made possible. Children get exposure. People receive structured guidance. Those who missed out on learning certain things earlier now have opportunities. Skill teachers' art instructors, music tutors, dance coaches find income and recognition today. The coaching culture has helped many. The coaching culture democratized mastery.

People today have greater access to learning art forms in depth and mastering them something that was once possible only for very focused or fortunate individuals. What used to be limited and difficult to access has now become far more open and reachable for everyone.

Earlier, we didn't learn rangoli because it was a skill, we learned because it was a ritual of the home. We didn't learn cooking to impress anyone, we learned because every home runs on shared participation.

We practised handwriting because letters and birthday cards mattered.

Today, children learn coding before they learn how to sew a button. They know how to operate an iPad before they know how to fold their own clothes. Lessons that once lived inside the walls of a home have moved outside into institutions. We replaced quiet teaching with formal training.

Children should grow up not only with skills they pay for, but also with skills they inherit. Not everything has to be structured. Not everything needs a certificate. Some things are best learned the old way - slowly, silently, naturally, while living life.

Yet life hasn't stopped teaching. Even now, children continue to learn from the world around them by observing, trying, failing, and trying again. What has shifted is the balance: structured lessons have grown more prominent, but the quiet, organic learning of everyday life still exists, often unnoticed.

It reminds of a time when learning wasn't purchased, it was inherited.
When creativity came from patience and surroundings, not from Pinterest boards.
When mistakes weren't erased, they became new patterns.
When the process mattered more than perfection.
When our memory was the only storage device we trusted.

Those little books we had were not just records of things.
They held rangoli patterns of dots and symmetry,

stamps gifted by friends and cousins, and cartoons copied carefully from Boomer wrappers.

They were proof of a different era of learning, one where curiosity was enough, patience was natural, and joy lived in the simple act of trying again.

Those little notebooks or the embroidered cloth pieces now rest in forgotten drawers, their pages yellowed, their corners bent, but their memories untouched by time or technology. They remind us of a world where learning flowed from life and not from logins.
Honestly, half the skills we learned weren't planned. They just happened.

Where curiosity was enough, and attention was the only skill required.

Some of us grew up tracing kolams with rice flour at dawn.
Some pressed snow angels into soft winter mornings.
Some drew hopscotch squares in chalk that faded with the first rain.
Some stitched embroidery, one loop and knot at a time.

Different places.
Different memories.
But the essence was the same, learning without pressure, without deadlines, without certificates.

We learned because life taught us, not because someone scheduled it.

We lived through a time before registrations, before coaching centres, before "Batch starts soon" and "Enrol now" became the gateway to every skill.

Today, children may scroll through thousands of designs online, search tutorials, download templates, but even now, when we walk past a neighbour's rangoli, some old instinct wakes up. The mind counts dots. The fingers trace invisible symmetry. The memory lives. Habits never left, it simply exists in a faster world.

Maybe someday, someone will find our old rangoli books, stamp albums, and hand-drawn cartoons, and wonder how we learned anything without Wi-Fi.
And maybe the answer will always be simple:
We learned from life, and it noticed us.

Chapter 17: From Textbooks to Visual Learning

Learning was once an exercise in patience, focus, and memory. Textbooks dominated the educational landscape, their pages filled with words, occasional diagrams, and structured chapters. Every concept required careful reading, imagination, and repeated practice. Understanding was built slowly, layer by layer. To grasp abstract ideas, learners had to rely on mental visualization, internal logic, and often, guidance from teachers who could translate words into examples.

For a long time, learning happened inside our own head. The textbook was the main tool in the classroom. It was often a thick, heavy thing with small print and hardly any colour. We knew the thrill of finding a rare coloured picture in a textbook; in a sea of grey text, it felt like discovering a hidden treasure. If a student in the 1970s or 80s wanted to understand how a volcano erupted or what a distant jungle looked like, they had to read the words.

In those days, the mind had to do all the work. When a book described "two roads diverged in a yellow wood," we had to close our eyes and build that picture ourself. We had to take the words on the page and turn them into a movie in our mind. It was hard work. We couldn't just sit back and watch; we had to actively create.

Because the books were often hard to understand, people were very important. Teachers, parents, and elders were the ones who unlocked the secrets. The teacher stood at the front of the room, covered in chalk dust, trying to explain complicated things with just their voice and a few drawings on the board. They were the bridge. We scribbled furiously to copy their diagrams, knowing the disappointment when the teacher erased the board too fast, wiping away the answer before we had captured it. They took the dry words and made them come alive.

At home, it was the same. If we wanted to know how to fix a bicycle, we didn't search the internet. We asked our dad or mom. Maybe they would tell us a story about it. There was a special respect for older people then because they held the knowledge in their heads, not on a server. The downside was that if our teacher or elders couldn't explain it well, we were stuck. But the upside was that we learned how to focus. We learned how to sit still, read deep, and really think.

Knowledge was linear and formal. Each chapter was a step, each paragraph a bridge. Mistakes in understanding could only be corrected through repetition or discussion. We recall the frustration of tearing pages from rough notebooks when a diagram went wrong or the ink smudged, the physical cost of perfection. The process was deliberate, measured, and sometimes frustrating. It required discipline, which made learning an achievement, but also limited participation to those willing to commit.

The change didn't happen all at once. It came slowly. First, it was the visual aids in the classroom: the charts, the pull-down maps, and then the overhead projector that hummed and made the room hot. These were the first steps away from just reading. We remember the fear during a projector malfunction when the whole class waited in the dim light, holding our breath while the teacher fiddled with the machine, hoping the lesson would resume.

Then came the internet and high-speed video, and everything changed forever. YouTube channels and educational apps dedicated to concept explanation exploded onto the scene. We moved from a world of text to a world of video.

This change was not simply about technology; it reflected a deeper understanding of how humans process information. Visual learning tapped into perception, intuition, and curiosity. Suddenly, learning became incredibly easy. Think about trying to learn how to tie a fancy tie or fix a leaky sink just by reading a manual. It's confusing. "Cross the left side over the right"-it's hard to picture. But now? We watch a ten-second video, and we see exactly how to do it.

The doors opened for everyone. Complicated math that used to scare people is now explained with beautiful animations that make it look like a game. Biology students don't have to imagine how cells divide; they can watch a perfect 3D animation of it. Apps allowed students to simulate physics experiments, explore interactive maps, or watch animated sequences that explained complex phenomena. Chemistry reactions that once had to be imagined could be watched safely on a screen.

But there is a catch. Because there is so much to watch, we have become "casual learners." In the old days, opening a textbook was an event. We sat at a desk, turned on a lamp, and focused. It was real work. Today, we learn in the cracks of our day. We watch a history video while waiting for the bus or learn a recipe while lying in bed.

Because the videos are so good, they can create an illusion of competence. Watching a master carpenter build a table on video makes us feel like we could build a table. We understand the story of it, but we haven't felt the difficulty of it. We miss the struggle. And that struggle is often what helps us remember things.

Furthermore, our attention is scattered. Educational videos now have to compete with funny cat videos and viral dances. To keep us watching, learning has to be entertaining. It has to be fast and flashy. We get the quick facts, but we might miss the deep meaning. We treat knowledge like a snack instead of a meal.

Ultimately, the integration of textbooks and visual tools has created a complementary relationship. Textbooks provide depth, structure, and context, while visual learning offers clarity, engagement, and immediacy. A student can read a description of a chemical reaction, observe it animated on a screen, and finally test the concept through a simulation.

The democratization of learning became evident. Knowledge is no longer confined to classrooms or those who can afford extensive resources. Anyone willing to engage can understand astronomy, economics, biology, or literature. The tools have evolved, but the pursuit of knowledge persists.

We have moved from a time where we had to use our imagination to see the world, to a time where the world is shown to us in bright, moving colours on a screen. This change has made learning easier for everyone, but it has also changed us. It has turned learning from a serious climb into a casual walk.

But we should remember what we left behind. That "mental muscle" we used to build, the one that turned words into worlds, is getting a bit weak. The quiet seriousness of a library has been replaced by the noise of the feed.

As we move forward, maybe the best way isn't to throw away the screens, but to remember the value of the books. We need the speed of the video to show us the world, but we still need the patience of the text to really understand it.

For those of us who grew up right in the middle of this change, we see things a little differently. We are the generation that started school with chalkboards and finished with laptops. We remember life before Google, but we are young enough to use it every day. Because we stood in both worlds, we value things that might seem strange now.

We value the **wait**. We remember waiting a week for a library book to arrive or waiting an hour for a single image to download. That waiting taught us that good things take time and that answers aren't always instant.

We value **memory**. We are the last generation that knew our best friend's home phone number by heart and could navigate to a distant relative's house using only landmarks and mental maps. We didn't have GPS to tell us every turn; we had to know the route. Today, we have outsourced that memory to the cloud, but we cherish the feeling of simply knowing.

We value the **physical world**. We love the smell of old paper, the weight of a book in our hands, and the feeling of writing with a pen. We know that screens can feel cold and flat, and that sometimes, touching the page makes the words feel more real.

But mostly, we value the **miracle of access**. Because we remember the struggle of the old days, we don't take the internet for granted. We value the speed of today more than anyone else because we know exactly what it was like to go without it. To us, the magic rectangle in our pocket is still a gift, not just a habit.

We remember a time before "Watch this video to learn", and maybe that memory is what keeps us grounded in a world that moves too fast.

Chapter 18: Conclusion

As we move through life, it becomes easy to forget how much the world has changed in such a short span of time.

We adapt so quickly that yesterday's miracles become today's routines, and the small wonders of the past fade into background memories.

This book was an attempt to pause that rush; to look back at the world we came from and understand how it shaped the world we live in now.

This ability to move between worlds is our strength. It gives us perspective, balance, and a kind of emotional intelligence that comes from living through contrast.

We are not torn between past and present; we are stitched by both. The past is a warm echo, the present a fast rhythm, and we, somewhere in between carry the ability to cherish slowness while adapting to speed.

As you close this book, I hope it leaves you with a quiet warmth, not just the nostalgia of the past, but an awareness of how much of that past still lives inside you. The simplicity, the slowness, the togetherness may no longer surround us in the same way, but they have shaped how we think, love, remember, and move through life.

The world will continue to change. New technologies will arrive, old habits will fade, and the rhythm of life will grow faster. But the memories we carry from the 90s will always remind us of who we were before the pace picked up, and why a part of us still longs for that gentler world.

This book is not meant to preserve the past, nor to hold on to it. It is simply a reminder.
A reminder that our childhoods were real and meaningful.
A reminder that our transitions shaped us more than we realise.
A reminder that nostalgia is not about going back, but about understanding where we come from, and carrying its lessons forward with intention.

Thank you for walking through these memories with me.
May these pages help you revisit your own, and may that warmth stay with you, quietly, gently, and fully alive, long after this final page.

About
Soumya Viswanathan

Soumya Viswanathan has always had a natural inclination toward writing essays and reflective pieces. She is a keen observer of life's subtle details. Her writing reflects a deep appreciation for simplicity, shared experiences, and the quieter moments that shaped everyday living.

She approaches nostalgia not as a longing for the past, but as a way of understanding how early experiences continue to influence who we become. The patience, togetherness, and warmth still live within us, even as the world accelerates.

The 90s, The Last Offline Generation is both a personal reflection and a collective memory, an attempt to pause, reflect, and honour a generation shaped by the quiet rhythms of the 1990s, a time when life moved slower and moments were lived more fully. Having lived through the shift from an offline childhood to an online adulthood, she writes from the space between memory and modern life.

Writing, for her, is a form of quiet reflection. It creates space to pause, observe, and make sense of emotional shifts, social expectations, and personal transformations.

She often writes about everyday life, unspoken roles, and the silent adjustments people make in order to belong, to care, and to endure. These experiences are explored with honesty and restraint, leaving room for readers to recognize their own lives within the words.

Her style values clarity over complexity and depth over decoration. She prefers a straightforward, grounded approach, rooted in lived experience rather than abstraction.

She writes not to instruct or impress, but to connect—to remind readers that their unnoticed thoughts, quiet struggles, and half-remembered moments carry meaning. If her writing feels familiar, it speaks from shared ground and common experience.

Through her work, she gently traces the invisible threads—reminding readers that who they were continues to shape who they are becoming, even as the world moves forward. She believes that even the smallest experiences carry the weight of stories worth telling.

more about her…

Her previous work, **She, Inside Her New Walls**, is a poetry collection that delves into a woman's journey through the emotional terrains navigated after marriage – where routines, meals and dreams are quietly reshaped. Rooted in collective experiences she has known, observed, and carried.

www.ingramcontent.com/pod-product-compliance
Lightning Source LLC
Chambersburg PA
CBHW031522180726
48282CB00056B/217
9789355923301